MI
on i
STATIONS
of the **CROSS**

John Henry Newman

*All booklets are published
thanks to the generosity of the supporters
of the Catholic Truth Society*

CATHOLIC TRUTH SOCIETY

PUBLISHERS TO THE HOLY SEE

Contents

All rights reserved. Revised edition 2015; first published 1927 by The Incorporated Catholic Truth Society, 40-46 Harleyford Road London SE11 5AY Tel: 020 7640 0042 Fax: 020 7640 0046. © 2015 The Incorporated Catholic Truth Society.

ISBN 978 1 78469 029 8

THE VALUE OF THE STATIONS
OF THE CROSS

The Stations, or Way, of the Cross, traditionally began two thousand years ago when the Blessed Virgin followed in the bloodstained footsteps of her Divine Son after the Crucifixion on Good Friday. She followed the "Via Dolorosa" taken by Christ through Jerusalem and up Mount Calvary, stopping at particular points, which are now associated with the fourteen Stations of the Cross found in Catholic churches. This devotion gradually developed during Church history, but particularly from the end of seventeenth century onwards.

The great value of the Stations lies in the fact that they allow believers to make a pilgrimage in spirit, and thus re-live the events of Christ's Passion and Death, starting with his condemnation before Pilate, and ending with his burial in Joseph of Arimathea's tomb. By passing from station to station, and reciting prayers and meditating on Christ's sufferings, the believer becomes one with Him in his sufferings and death.

The Church has highly indulgenced the Stations of the Cross as an encouragement for the Faithful to meditate on Christ's sufferings, in a devotion which inspires us to take up our cross and follow Him. The great Fathers, Doctors and Saints have been assiduous in recommending meditation on the Passion of Christ as the surest way to come close to Christ and imitate him.

According to St Augustine, one tear shed while meditating upon the Passion is of more value than a year spent in fasting on bread and water, or in going on a pilgrimage to Jerusalem.

St Bonaventure said that those who meditate on the Passion are "divinised," that is, made God-like, and that the wounds of Christ are capable of melting the hardest of hearts. St Alphonsus Ligouri said that the Saints attained their courage to bear their sufferings in the sufferings of Jesus crucified, and that when we meditate on the Passion of Christ we are inflamed with love of God and come to realise how much the Saviour loved us.

With their focus on the individual's part in causing the Passion of Christ, through our sins, Cardinal Newman's Stations of the Cross are written in the spirit of the great spiritual masters of the past, but at the same time they are positive and uplifting in their focus on the love and mercy of God.

JOHN HENRY NEWMAN

John Henry Newman was born in London in February 1801, and died at Edgbaston in Birmingham in August 1890. He became one of the best known religious figures in England from the 1830s onwards and was eventually made a Cardinal by Pope Leo XIII in 1879.

Newman was converted from Anglicanism in the 1840s, having been a leader of the Oxford Movement, which was made up of Anglicans wishing to reform the Established Church. His studies of the works of the Church Fathers, amongst other things, convinced him that Anglicanism was not the *via media* or middle position between Protestantism and the Catholic Church, and this led him to embrace Catholicism. Thus he was received into the Church by Blessed Dominic Barberi, a Passionist, in October 1845, at Littlemore near Oxford.

Newman was a noted writer whose work has continued to be very influential, with his autobiography *Apologia pro Vita Sua*, and his *Grammar of Assent* being particularly popular. His best known theological work, though, is his *Essay on the Development of Christian Doctrine*, which has exerted a great influence on the Catholic theology of doctrinal development. He also wrote the poem *The Dream of Gerontius*, which was set to music by Elgar, and various hymns.

He was responsible, too, for the founding of the first Catholic University in Ireland, which eventually became

University College Dublin, and also for the introduction of the Oratorian Order of St Philip Neri into England, at Edgbaston in Birmingham, and in London.

Newman is one of the very few non-Saints to be quoted in the *Catechism of the Catholic Church*, and the extensive references to his work attest to the deep influence he has had on the development of theology in the Church in recent times. He was in favour of the empowerment of the laity in the Church, especially in the area of the intellectual life of Catholics, and in this respect was far ahead of his time.

When he became a Cardinal, he said the focus of his life had been his opposition to religious liberalism, that is, the idea that sentiment or opinion in religious matters were more important than the truth.

He died in August 1890, of pneumonia, at the Birmingham Oratory: the pall over the coffin bore his motto as a Cardinal, *Cor ad cor loquitur* ("Heart speaks to heart").

Cardinal Newman was declared Venerable by Pope St John Paul II in January 1991, and beatified by Pope Benedict XVI during a visit to the United Kingdom in September 2010.

THE FOURTEEN STATIONS

Begin with an Act of Contrition

O my God, because you are so good,
I am very sorry that I have sinned against you
and by the help of your grace
I will not sin again.

For each Station open with:
V. *We adore you, O Christ, and we bless you.*
R. *Because by your holy Cross you have redeemed the world.*

For each Station conclude with:
Our Father, Hail Mary, Glory be to the Father.

V. *Have mercy on us, O Lord.*
R. *Have mercy on us.*

May the souls of the faithful departed, through the mercy of God, rest in peace. Amen.

THE FIRST STATION
JESUS IS CONDEMNED TO DEATH

Leaving the house of Caiaphas, and dragged before Pilate and Herod, mocked, beaten, and spit upon, His back torn with scourges, His head crowned with thorns, Jesus, who on the last day will judge the world, is Himself condemned by unjust judges to a death of ignominy and torture.

Jesus is condemned to death. His death-warrant is signed, and who signed it but I, when I committed my first mortal sins? My first mortal sins, when I fell away from the state of grace into which You did place me by baptism; these it was that became Your death-warrant, O Lord. The innocent suffered for the guilty. Those sins of mine were the voices which cried out, 'Let Him be crucified.' That willingness and delight of heart with which I committed them was the consent which Pilate gave to this clamorous multitude. And the hardness of heart which followed upon them, my disgust, my despair, my proud impatience, my obstinate resolve to sin on, the love of sin which took possession of me - what were these contrary and impetuous feelings but the blows and the blasphemies with which the fierce soldiers and the populace received You, thus carrying out the sentence which Pilate had pronounced?

THE SECOND STATION

JESUS RECEIVES HIS CROSS

A strong, and therefore heavy, Cross, for it is strong enough to bear Him on it when He arrives at Calvary, is placed upon His torn shoulders. He receives it gently and meekly, no, with gladness of heart, for it is to be the salvation of mankind.

True; but recollect, that heavy Cross is the weight of our sins. As it fell upon His neck and shoulders, it came down with a shock. Alas! what a sudden, heavy weight have I laid upon You, O Jesus! And though in the calm and clear foresight of Your mind - for You see all things - You were fully prepared for it, yet Your feeble frame tottered under it when it dropped down upon You. Ah! how great a misery is it that I have lifted up my hand against my God! How could I ever imagine He would forgive me unless He had Himself told us that He underwent His bitter Passion in order that he might forgive us. I acknowledge, O Jesus, in the anguish and agony of my heart, that it was my sins that struck You on the face, that bruised Your sacred arms, that tore Your flesh with iron rods, that nailed You to the Cross, and let You slowly die upon it.

THE THIRD STATION

JESUS FALLS THE FIRST TIME
BENEATH THE CROSS

Jesus, bowed down under the weight and the length of the unwieldy Cross, which trailed after Him, slowly sets forth on His way, amid the mockeries and insults of the crowd. His agony in the Garden itself was sufficient to exhaust Him; but it was only the first of a multitude of sufferings. He sets off with His whole heart, but His limbs fail Him, and He falls. Yes, it is as I feared. Jesus, the strong and mighty Lord, has found for the moment our sins stronger than Himself. He falls, yet He bore the load for a while; He tottered, but He bore up and walked onwards.

What, then, made Him give way? I say, I repeat, it is an intimation and a memory to you, O my soul, of your falling back into mortal sin. I repented of the sins of my youth, and went on well for a time; but at length a new temptation came, when I was off my guard, and I suddenly fell away. Then all my good habits seemed to go at once; they were like a garment which is stripped off, so quickly and utterly did grace depart from me. And at that moment I looked at my Lord, and behold He had fallen down, and I covered my face with my hands, and remained in a state of great confusion.

THE FOURTH STATION
JESUS MEETS HIS MOTHER

Jesus rises; though wounded by His fall, He journeys on, with His Cross still on His shoulders. He is bent down; but at one place, looking up, He sees His Mother. For an instant they just see each other, and He goes forward. Mary would rather have had all His sufferings herself, could that have been, than not have known what they were by ceasing to be near Him. He, too, gained a refreshment, as from some soothing and grateful breath of air, to see her sad smile amid the sights and the sounds which were about Him. She had known Him beautiful and glorious, with the freshness of divine innocence and peace upon His countenance; now she saw Him so changed and deformed that she could scarce have recognised Him, save for the penetrating, stirring, peace-inspiring look He gave her. Still, He was now carrying the load of the world's sins, and, all-holy though He was, He carried the image of them on His very face. He looked like some outcast or outlaw who had frightful guilt upon Him. He had been made sin for us, who knew no sin; not a feature, not a limb, but spoke of guilt, of a curse, of punishment, of agony. Oh, what a meeting of Son and Mother! Yet there was a mutual comfort, for there was a mutual sympathy. Jesus and Mary - do they forget that Passiontide through all eternity?

THE FIFTH STATION

SIMON OF CYRENE HELPS JESUS TO CARRY THE CROSS

At length His strength fails utterly, and He is unable to proceed. The executioners stand perplexed. What are they to do? How is He to get to Calvary? Soon they see a stranger who seems strong and active - Simon of Cyrene. They seize on him, and compel him to carry the Cross with Jesus. The sight of the Sufferer pierces the man's heart. Oh, what a privilege! O happy soul, elect of God! He takes the part assigned to him with joy.

This came of Mary's intercession. He prayed not for Himself, except that He might drink the full chalice of suffering and do His Father's will; but she showed herself a mother by following Him with her prayers, since she could help Him in no other way. She then sent this stranger to help Him. It was she who led the soldiers to see that they might not be too fierce with Him. Sweet Mother, do the same for us. Pray for us always, Holy Mother of God, pray for us, whatever be our cross, as we pass along on our way. Pray for us, and we shall rise again though we have fallen. Pray for us when sorrow, anxiety, or sickness comes upon us. Pray for us when we are prostrate under the power of temptation, and send some faithful servant of yours to help us. And in the world to come, if found worthy to expiate our sins in purgatory, send some good angel to give us a time of refreshment. Pray for us, Holy Mother of God.

THE SIXTH STATION
JESUS AND VERONICA

As Jesus toils along up the hill, covered with the sweat of death, a woman makes her way through the crowd, and wipes His face with her veil. In reward of her piety the cloth retains the impression of the Sacred Countenance upon it.

The relief which a mother's tenderness secured is not yet all Our Lady did. Her prayers sent Veronica as well as Simon - Simon to do a man's work, Veronica to do the part of a woman. The devout servant of Jesus did what she could. As Magdalen had poured the ointment at the feast, so Veronica now offered Him her veil in His passion. 'Ah,' she said, 'would I could do more! Why have I not the strength of Simon, to take part in the burden of the Cross? But men only can serve the Great High Priest, now that He is celebrating the solemn act of sacrifice.' O Jesus! let us one and all minister to You according to our places and powers. And as You did accept from Your followers refreshment in Your hour of trial, so give to us the support of Your grace when we are hard pressed by our foe. I feel I cannot bear up against temptation, weariness, despondency, and sin. I say to myself, what is the good of being religious? I shall fall, O my dear Saviour, I shall certainly fall, unless You renew for me my vigour like the eagle's, and breathe life into me by the soothing application and the touch of the holy Sacraments which You have appointed.

THE SEVENTH STATION
JESUS FALLS A SECOND TIME

The pain of His wounds and the loss of blood increasing at every step of His way, again His limbs fail Him, and He falls on the ground.

What has He done to deserve all this? This is the reward received by the long-expected Messiah from the Chosen People, the Children of Israel. I know what to answer. He falls because I have fallen. I have fallen again. I know well that without Your grace, O Lord, I could not stand; and I imagined that I had kept closely to Your Sacraments; yet in spite of my going to Mass and to my duties, I am lacking grace again. Why is it but because I have lost my devotional spirit, and have come to Your holy decrees in a cold, formal way, without inward affection. I became lukewarm, tepid. I thought the battle of life was over, and became secure. I had no lively faith, no sight of spiritual things. I came to church from habit, and because I thought others would observe it. I ought to be a new creature, I ought to live by faith, hope, and charity; but I thought more of this world than the world to come - and finally I forgot that I was a servant of God, and followed the broad way that leads to destruction, not the narrow way which leads to life. And thus I fell from You.

THE EIGHTH STATION
JESUS COMFORTS THE WOMEN OF JERUSALEM

At the sight of the sufferings of Jesus the holy women are so pierced with grief that they cry out and bewail Him, careless of what happens to them by doing so. Jesus, turning to them, said, 'Daughters of Jerusalem, weep not over Me, but weep for yourselves and for your children.'

Ah! can it be, O Lord, that I shall prove one of those sinful children for whom You ask their mothers to weep? 'Weep not for Me,' He said, 'for I am the Lamb of God, and am making atonement by My own will for the sins of the world. I am suffering now, but I shall triumph; and, when I triumph, those souls for whom I am dying, will either be my dearest friends or my deadliest enemies.' Is it possible? O my Lord, can I grasp the terrible thought that You really did weep for me - weep for me, as You wept over Jerusalem? Is it possible that I am one of the reprobate, the lost? Possible that I shall lose by Your passion and death, not gain by it? Oh, do not withdraw from me. I am in a very bad way. I have so much evil in me. I have so little of an earnest, brave spirit to set against that evil. O Lord, what will become of me? It is so difficult for me to drive away the Evil Spirit from my heart. You alone can effectually cast him out.

THE NINTH STATION
AGAIN, A THIRD TIME,
JESUS FALLS

Jesus had now reached almost to the top of Calvary; but, before He had reached the very spot where he was to be crucified, again He fell, and was again dragged up and hounded onwards by the brutal soldiery.

We are told in Holy Scripture of three falls of Satan, the Evil Spirit. The first was in the beginning; the second, when the Gospel and the Kingdom of Heaven were preached to the world; the third will be at the end of all things. The first is told us by St John the Evangelist. He says: 'There was a great battle in heaven. Michael and his angels fought with the dragon, and the dragon fought, and his angels. And they prevailed not, neither was their place found any more in heaven. And that great dragon was cast out, the old serpent, who is called the devil and Satan.' The second fall, at the time of the Gospel, is spoken of by our Lord when He says, 'I saw Satan, like lightning, falling from heaven.' And the third by the same St John: 'There came down fire from God out of heaven, …and the devil…was cast into the pool of fire and brimstone.' These three falls - the past, the present, and the future - the Evil Spirit had in mind when he moved Judas to betray our Lord. This was just his hour. Our Lord, when He was seized, said to His enemies, 'This is your hour and the power of darkness.' Satan knew his time was short, and thought he might use it to good effect.

But - little dreaming that he would be acting in behalf of the world's redemption, which our Lord's passion and death were to work out - in revenge, and, as he thought, in triumph, he struck Him once, he struck Him twice, he struck Him three times, each successive time a heavier blow. The weight of the Cross, the barbarity of the soldiers and the crowd, were but his instruments. O Jesus, the only-begotten Son of God, the Word Incarnate, we praise, adore, and love You for Your ineffable condescension, even to allowing Yourself thus for a time to fall into the hands and under the power of the Enemy of God and man, in order thereby to save us from being his servants and companions for eternity.

An Alternative Reflection

This is the worst fall of the three. His strength has for a while utterly failed Him, and it is some time before the barbarous soldiers can bring Him to. Ah! it was His anticipation of what was to happen to me. I get worse and worse. He sees the end from the beginning. He was thinking of me all the time He dragged Himself along, up the hill of Calvary. He saw that I should fall again in spite of all former warnings and former assistance. He saw that I should become secure and self-confident, and that my enemy would then assail me with some new temptation, to which I never thought I should be exposed. I thought my weakness lay all on one particular side which I knew. I did not dream that I was not strong on the other. And so Satan came down on my unguarded side, and got the better of me from my self-trust and self-satisfaction. I was wanting in humility. I thought no harm would come on me; I thought I had outlived the danger of sinning; I thought it was an easy thing to get to heaven, and I was not watchful. It was my pride, and so I fell a third time.

THE TENTH STATION

JESUS IS STRIPPED OF HIS GARMENTS

At length He has arrived at the place of sacrifice, and they begin to prepare Him for the Cross. His garments are torn from His bleeding body, and He, the Holy of Holies, stands exposed to the gaze of the coarse and scoffing multitude.

O You who in Your Passion were stripped of all your clothes, and held up to the curiosity and mockery of the rabble, strip me of myself here and now, that in the Last Day I will not be ashamed before men and angels. You endured the shame on Calvary, that I might be spared the shame at the Judgement. You had nothing to be ashamed of personally, and the shame which You did feel was because You had taken on You man's nature. When they took from You Your garments, those innocent limbs of Yours were but objects of humble and loving adoration to the highest Seraphim. They stood around in speechless awe, wondering at Your beauty, and they trembled at Your infinite self-abasement. But I, O Lord, how shall I appear if You shall hold me up hereafter to be gazed upon, stripped of that robe of grace which is Yours, and seen in my own personal life and nature? O how hideous I am in myself, even in my best condition. Even when I am cleansed from my mortal sins, what disease and corruption is seen even in my venial sins. How shall I be fit for the society of angels, how for Your presence, until You burn this foul leprosy away in the fire of Purgatory?

ELEVENTH STATION
JESUS IS NAILED TO THE CROSS

The Cross is laid on the ground, and Jesus stretched upon it, and then, swaying heavily to and fro, it is, after much exertion, jerked into the hole ready to receive it. Or, as others think, it is set upright, and Jesus is raised up and fastened to it. As the savage executioners drive in the huge nails, He offers Himself to the Eternal Father as a ransom for the world. The blows are struck - the blood gushes forth.

Yes, they set up the Cross on high, and they placed a ladder against it, and, having stripped Him of His garments, made Him mount it. With His hands feebly grasping its sides and cross-woods, and His feet slowly, uncertainly, with much effort, with many slips, mounting up, the soldiers propped Him on each side or He would have fallen. When He reached the projection where His sacred feet were to be, He turned round with sweet modesty and gentleness towards the fierce rabble, stretching out His arms, as if He would embrace them. Then He lovingly placed the backs of His hands close against the transverse beam, waiting for the executioners to come with their sharp nails and heavy hammers to dig into the palms of His hands, and to fasten them securely to the wood. There He hung, a perplexity to the multitude, a terror to evil spirits, the wonder, the awe, yet the joy, the adoration, of the holy angels.

THE TWELFTH STATION
JESUS DIES UPON THE CROSS

Jesus hung on the Cross for three hours. During this time He prayed for His murderers, promised Paradise to the penitent robber, and committed His Blessed Mother to the guardianship of St John. Then all was finished, and He bowed His head and gave up His Spirit.

The worst is over. The Holiest is dead and departed. The most tender, the most affectionate, the holiest of the sons of men is gone. Jesus is dead, and with His death my sin shall die. I protest once for all, before men and angels, that sin shall no more have dominion over me. This Lent I make myself God's own for ever. The salvation of my soul shall be my first concern. With the aid of His grace I will create in me a deep hatred and sorrow for my past sins. I will try hard to detest sin, as much as I have ever loved it. Into God's hands I put myself, not by halves, but unreservedly. I promise You, O Lord, with the help of Your grace to keep out of the way of temptation, to avoid all occasions of sin, to turn at once from the voice of the Evil One, to be regular in my prayers, so to die to sin that You may not have died for me on the Cross in vain.

THE THIRTEENTH STATION

JESUS IS TAKEN FROM THE CROSS, AND LAID IN MARY'S BOSOM

The multitude have gone home; Calvary is left solitary and still, except that St John and the holy women are there. Then come Joseph of Arimathea and Nicodemus, and take down from the Cross the body of Jesus, and place it in the arms of Mary.

O Mary, at last you have possession of your Son. Now, when His enemies can do no more, they leave Him in contempt to you. As His unexpected friends perform their difficult work, you look on with inexpressible thoughts. Your heart is pierced with the sword of which Simeon spoke. O Mother most sorrowful; yet in your sorrow there is a still greater joy. The joy in prospect strengthened you to stand by Him as He hung upon the Cross; much more now, without swooning, without trembling, do you receive Him to your arms and on your lap. Now you are supremely happy as having Him, though He comes to you not as He went from you. He went from your home, O Mother of God, in the strength and beauty of His manhood, and He comes back to you dislocated, torn to pieces, mangled, dead. Yet, O Blessed Mary, you are happier in the hour of woe than on the day of the marriage feast, for then He was leaving you, and now in the future, as a risen Saviour, He will be separated from you no more.

THE FOURTEENTH STATION
JESUS IS LAID IN THE TOMB

But for a short three days, for a day and a half - Mary then must give Him up. He is not yet risen. His friends and servants take Him from her, and place Him in an honourable tomb. They close it safely, till the hour comes for His resurrection.

Lie down and sleep in peace in the calm grave for a little while, dear Lord, and then wake up for your everlasting reign. We, like the faithful women, will watch around You, for all our treasure, all our life, is lodged with You. And, when our turn comes to die, grant, sweet Lord, that we may sleep calmly too, the sleep of the just. Let us sleep peacefully for the brief interval between death and the general resurrection. Guard us from the enemy, save us from the pit. Let our friends remember us and pray for us, O dear Lord. Let Masses be said for us, so that the pains of Purgatory, so much deserved by us and therefore so truly welcomed by us, may be over with little delay. Give us seasons of refreshment there; wrap us round with holy dreams and soothing contemplations, while we gather strength to ascend to the heavens. And then let our faithful guardian angels help us up the glorious ladder, reaching from earth to heaven, which Jacob saw in vision. And when we reach the everlasting gates, let them open upon us with the music of angels; and let St Peter receive us, and Our Lady, the glorious Queen of Saints, embrace us, and bring us to You, and to Your Eternal Father, and to Your Co-equal Spirit, Three Persons, One God, to reign with Them for ever and ever.

Our Father, Hail Mary, Glory be to the Father

Let us Pray: *God who by the Precious Blood of Your only-begotten Son did sanctify the Standard of the Cross, grant, we beseech You, that we who rejoice in the glory of the same holy Cross may at all times and places rejoice in Your protection through the same Christ, our Lord.*

End with one Our Father, Hail Mary, and Glory be for the intentions of the Holy Father.

ADDITIONAL PRAYERS AND EXAMINATION OF CONSCIENCE

The following examination of conscience can help us to measure our lives by the objective standard of Christ's teaching. We may also consider more generally how we may have failed in our lives to live fully as disciples of Christ.

Sins against God

Have I rejected my faith, refused to find out more about it?

Have I forgotten my daily prayers or said them badly?

Have I experimented with the occult or put my trust in fortune tellers or horoscopes?

Have I blasphemed against God or used bad language?

Have I shown disrespect for holy things, places or people?

Have I missed Mass on Sundays or Holydays through my own fault?

Have I let myself be distracted at Mass or distracted others?

Have I received Holy Communion in a state of mortal sin?

Have I received Holy Communion without proper reverence, care or thanksgiving?

Sins against myself and others

Have I been impatient, angry or jealous?

Have I brooded over injuries or refused to forgive?

Have I taken part in or encouraged abortion, the destruction of human embryos, euthanasia or any other means of taking human life?

Have I been verbally or physically violent to others?

Have I been racist in my thoughts, words or deeds?

Have I hurt anyone by speaking badly about them?

Have I betrayed confidences without good cause or revealed things simply to hurt others?

Have I judged others rashly?

Have I been drunk or used illegal drugs?

Have I driven dangerously or inconsiderately?

Have I spoken in an obscene way?

Have I looked at obscene pictures, films or books?

Have I been involved in any impure behaviour on my own or with someone else?

Have I been vain, proud, selfish or self-seeking?

Have I told lies to excuse myself, to hurt others or to make myself look more important?

Have I stolen anything?

Have I failed to contribute to the support of the Church in proportion to my means?

Have I been disobedient, rude or insolent to those in authority over me?

Have I been harsh, overbearing or sarcastic to those under my authority?

Have I cheated my employers or employees?

Have I misused or damaged the property of others?

Have I set my heart greedily on possessing things?

Have I given scandal or bad example?

Have I been lazy at my work, study or domestic duties?

Have I been jealous of others – of their looks, their popularity, their good work?

Have I encouraged others to do wrong in any way?

For spouses

Have I neglected to foster the warmth of my love and affection for my spouse?

Have I prolonged disagreements through resentment or failing to apologise when I have been in the wrong?

Have I mistreated my spouse verbally, emotionally or physically?

Have I used artificial means of birth control?

Have I been unfaithful to my spouse in any way?

For parents

Have I neglected to teach my children to pray?

Have I neglected the religious education of my children?

Have I failed to bring my children to Sunday Mass?

Have I argued with my spouse in front of my children?

Have I failed to exercise vigilance over what my children read, see on television or on the internet?

Have I been harsh or overbearing to my children?

Have I neglected my children's welfare in any way?

For young people

Have I been disobedient to my parents?

Have I been unhelpful at home?

Have I failed to try to understand my parents and talk with them?

Have I upset the peace of my home for selfish reasons?

Have I lost control when I have been angry?

Have I sulked or been sarcastic instead of asking for help?

Have I failed to work properly at school?

Have I treated teachers or other adults with disrespect?

Have I played unfairly at games or sports?

Have I taken part in fights?

PRAYERS OF CARDINAL NEWMAN

O God, give me grace at this time duly to confess my sins before you, and truly to repent of them. Blot out of your book, gracious Lord, all my manifold acts of sin committed against you. Forgive me all my wanderings in prayer, my sins of omission, my deliberate sins against conscience. Give me eyes to see what is right, and a heart to follow it, and strength to perform it; and grant that I may in all things press forward in the work of sanctification and ever do your will, and at length through your mercy attain to the glories of your everlasting kingdom through Jesus Christ our Lord.

A Prayer of Trust in God

God has created me to do him some definite service; he has committed some work to me which he has not committed to another. I have my mission - I may never know it in this life, but I shall be told it in the next. I am a link in a chain, a bond of connection between persons. He has not created me for naught. I shall do good, I shall do his work; I shall be a preacher of truth in my own place, while not intending it, if I do but keep his commandments and serve him in my calling.

A Prayer for Christ's Forbearance

O Jesu, does any number of falls and relapses vanquish the faithfulness and endurance of your compassion? You forgive not only seven times, but to seventy times seven. And such you are all over the earth, even to the end - forgiving, sparing, forbearing, waiting, though sinners are ever provoking you: pitying and taking into account their ignorance, visiting all men, all your enemies, with the gentle pleadings of your grace, day after day, year after year, up to the hour of their death. Bear with me in spite of my waywardness, perverseness, and ingratitude. Only give me your grace. Then I shall have happy days in your presence.

A Prayer to Bear Suffering Well

My great God, you have humbled yourself and have been lifted up upon the Cross! Though I am not fit to ask you for suffering as a gift, at least I will beg of you grace to meet suffering well, when you in your love and wisdom bring it upon me. Let me bear pain, reproach, disappointment, slander, anxiety, suspense, when it comes. I wish to bear insult meekly, and to return good for evil. I wish to humble myself in all things, and to be silent when I am ill used, and to be patient when sorrow or pain is prolonged, and all for the love of you, and your Cross, knowing that in this way I shall gain the promise of this life and of the next.

A Prayer of Surrender

My Lord and Saviour, in your arms I am safe; keep me and I have nothing to fear; give me up and I have nothing to hope for. I pray you not to make me rich, I pray you not to make me very poor; but I leave it all to you, because you know and I do not. If you bring pain or sorrow on me, give me grace to bear it well. If you give me health and strength and success in this world, keep me ever on my guard lest these great gifts carry me away from you. Give me ever to aim at setting forth your glory; to live to and for you; to set a good example to all around me; give me to die just at that time and in that way which is most for your glory, and best for my salvation.

Prayer for Canonisation of Cardinal John Henry Newman

God our Father, you granted to your servant John Henry Newman wonderful gifts of nature and of grace, that he should be a spiritual light in the darkness of this world, an eloquent herald of the Gospel, and a devoted servant of the one Church of Christ. With confidence in his heavenly intercession, we make the following petition: *[here make your petition]*.

For his insight into the mysteries of the kingdom, his zealous defence of the teachings of the Church, and his priestly love for each of your children, we pray that he may soon be numbered among the canonised saints. We ask this through Christ our Lord.